Building Hardees Restaurants

Raymond E. Smith

Published by
Sanway International
91 E. Main Street
Inman, SC 29349
Email: raymondsmith864@yahoo.com

ii

Dedicated to

All employees who worked for
Spartan Food Systems

Table of Contents

Introduction

My construction experience began when my Dad was preaching and decided to build a church building in 1947 (I was 12 years old). He never had any experience in construction. This was a new experience for him.

The block mason was a farmer and about every day he would leave about noon to tend his crops.

One day my dad told him, "When you leave today, leave your tools here." Dad had been watching him very closely. He thought now is the time for me to try laying blocks.

When the mason showed up for work the next day he said, "Your work is as good as mine."

Dad worked alongside him and finished the job. This created an interest in him to become a contractor.

He was faced with several challenges.

He put an ad in the local newspaper and listed a Post Office number for contact. We didn't have a telephone. Someone contacted him and wanted a foundation for a house laid. Dad said, "You will have to come and get me because I don't have a car."

This was at the end of the Great Depression and everyone was struggling.

I worked with him on Saturdays. I learned to spread mortar with a small pointing trowel. I tried laying blocks, but they were too heavy. Back then blocks weighed 50 pounds each.

Soon I became stronger and more experienced and was laying blocks as good as anyone.

A couple years later Dad was called to come and replace a column that a car hit and knocked down. When he saw the job he first words were, "This is bricks and I don't lay brick. I only lay blocks. Since Dad didn't lay bricks, I didn't have any experienced either. As we were leaving I said, "Dad I can do that." He said, "If you think you can do it then you be the contractor."

This started my own company of contracting at age 14. Within three years I was building most anything with blocks and bricks. In the community where we lived, they were building a new service station. I applied for the contract of laying blocks.

The contractor explained, "At your age I don't know. There are a lot of angles where blocks will have to be cut. He agreed to think about it.

I visited the job every day to watch the progress. One day he said, Okay I am going to give you a shot at laying the blocks, but the work must be first quality. With confidence, I replied, "If my work does not please you, you don't owe anything." He felt better.

The work progressed well and he was pleased. At the end he recommended me to the oil company he was working for and they gave me other jobs. This led to another oil company in an-other town. I was building most service stations in the area.

This led to other opportunities in construction. With this experience I had the confidence to branch out into other areas.

We built a large warehouse that took several thousands blocks and about a month to complete. We built bank buildings and office buildings.

I was assisting my brother do the masonry on the home office for a new fast food franchisee of Hardees called, Spartan Food Systems. The job was getting near the end and I saw the opportunity to branch into another phase of construction.

My Big Opportunity

Chapter One
The Opportunity

Toward the end of the work day, the vice president of Spartan Food System came by the job to check progress. I saw my opportunity and I took a leap.

I introduced my self and asked if the company is hiring any new superintendents. He quickly answered, "Yes, we are expanding and need good people."

He asked me to come by the temporary office downtown and talk with the President. I was greeted by Jerry Richardson (who is now the owner of the Carolina Panthers Football Team). Richardson was very friendly and asked if I wanted something to drink. At first, I told him no but he insisted. I said, "Do you have a coke?" He answered, "I've got more cokes than anyone in town." He went to the Hardees next door and brought back a large fountain cup of coke.

He spent the next 30 to 40 minutes telling me about the company's history and plans for the future. I told him about my experience and ambitions in construction. I was hired immediately.

On the first day, I was assigned to work with a guy who was doing some maintenance work on some of the stores.

That evening I was told to bring extra clothes and go to Atlanta for a few days.

The job was at five forks which is the heart of Atlanta. This was Spartans first store in a downtown setting. They were renovating an old building to build the Hardees. We first had to build a barricade at the sidewalk to protect pedestrians. One of the things that stood out about the job was there was no parking except parking garages and lots. Even trucks delivering materials had to pay to stop and unload.

We worked there for a week and I was assigned to assist another superintendent in remodeling an existing store. As it turned out the other guy was new and I had much more experience than he.

This job called for totally remodeling an old pagoda-style building with walk-up window service.

This was the first store Spartan owned; on Kennedy Street in Spartanburg.

Quickly the vice president, Jay Hammond recognized my potential and the other guy was assigned to food service.

As this job was completing, Hammond told me that he wanted me to go to Charlotte and build a new building. This was great news for me.

The first thing I did was to go to the last store that was built and pick up an office trailer. While cleaning it out I noticed a calendar with days marked off. I inquired and learned that that is the number of days it took to build the building. I counted and there were 90 days marked off.

I analyzed the work to be done and felt like I could beat his record.

This store was to be built in the parking lot of a shopping center. Using steel rods we drove them through the asphalt to lay out the corners of the building.

I chalked the outline of the ditch for the founda-tion. We dug the trenches through the asphalt by hand. Laborers gathered near downtown on Mintstreet (the exact location where the Carolina Panthers stadium was build).

When the equipment was installed we called for an inspection. The inspector was not pleased with the hood and exhaust system. He said, "The joints in the metal had to be welded and the hood had to have a UL label.

This presented two challenges they no one expected. Both were next to impossible.

The hood was built by a local independent fabricator and it would take years to get a UL approval from the government.

It would be impossible for a welder to get inside of a 10" by 14" exhaust duct system to weld the joints.

Olin Thompson, the project manager set out to solve the problems. First he bought a tube of liquid steel and caulked the joints as high as he could reach.

When it dried it appeared to be welded.

Then, he went to a store that sold small appliances and peeled off a UL label. Went this was done we called for another inspection. Everything was approved.

Other than that the job progressed very well. Getting near the end Hammond came by and told me my next assignment was to completely remodel a store across town. The store was originally a different fast food store.

We went over and took some measurements. He asked if I could draw the floor plan. I told him that though I could. He drew the idea of what it should look like on a paper bag.

Several days later he came by to see how I was doing with the floor plan. I not only drew a floor plan but wall section and roof plan. He was pleased and said that he would see what the city would say about it.

A few hours later while I was very busy with finishing details of the building when the phone rang. The voice on the other end said, "I want to speak to the architect." I said, "There is no architect here you have the wrong number." He insisted, "I know I have the right number." I was getting a little agitated when he said, "This is Jay Hammond." I was relieved. He said, "I walked the plan through every phase of city planning, zoning, and building. Your plan was approved."

This was great news. He said, "When you finish there move everything to the other location and start anytime."

When finishing the building, we counted the days marked off the calendar and there were 71 days. This excited everyone at the home office because they saved construction money and got the store opened sooner.

This started a contest to see who could build a store in the fewest amount of days. We received a bonus for each day saved. I held the winning number of days

Stores in Charlotte

Chapter Two
Stores in Charlotte

The remodeling job had some new challenges. Hammond and Thompson were spending most of their time in East Tennessee where several new stores were being built.

While thinking about the stores in TN. When they got the permit for the store in Johnson City the inspector explained that the city does not have a storm sewer system. Each building is responsible for their own rainwater. They had to bore a three-foot hole in the parking lot, 80 feet deep. It was filled with gravel to absorb the water.

Back to Charlotte.

This job was on Freedom Drive.

The building was originally a Jack In The Box Restaurant. The design was completely different from the Pagoda Hardees building. It had a tall steep roof over part of the building and a flat roof over the other.

I was left to work out the details as I went along. I drew the design of the steel package and wrote all the specifications. I carried it to the steel company. After looking over it and reading the specs. He said, "Your company sure has a good steel engineer. Boy, did I feel good. First, I was called an architect and now an engineer.

We worked long hours at night to avoid closing the store for business.

When I was ready for light fixtures they were not delivered. I called my brother in Johnson City, TN and asked if he had any. He told me his were already delivered, but he is not ready to use them. He agreed for me to come and get them and replaced them when mine were delivered. After working a full day and part of the night, I drove from Charlotte to Johnson City and picked up the fixtures. I got home in time to sleep a couple hours before leaving to go back to Charlotte.

When this job was finished I went to Independence Blvd. to remodel another old Hardees building.

There were times that it was difficult to get our usual contractors because of so many stores being built in TN and AL.

When I was ready for the tile contractors they sent a Skelton crew. We were experimenting with a new color scheme with tile in the dining areas.

There were a lot of red tiles. The tile company didn't order enough of the red tiles. The crew said they would come back after the tile was delivered.

I called the tile manufacturer in California and they told me the red tile was the most difficult to manufacture. This put my schedule behind, temporarily.

When the tile came I called the contractor. They said it would be several days and maybe as much as two weeks before they could come back.

I had developed the policy of warning a contractor, "If you don't show up I'll hire another contractor to replace you." I couldn't use that this time because this contractor did all the tile jobs for Spartan.

I waited a couple days. I decided to start laying the tile myself. I had never attempted to do tile work. When they finally came, a lot of the walls were finished. They said that my work was as good as theirs.

Near the finish of this job, I was assigned to remodel the store in Rock Hill. One day while checking the Rock Hill job Mr. Hammond and Mr. Richardson came by to see how the job was progressing. They invited me to go to lunch with them. This was a real treat.

Dealing with Brick Masons

Chapter Three
Dealing With Masons

Another challenge happened while building stores in Charlotte. This job was different than all the other stores. This was a new experiment; a cafeteria.

When the masons finished laying the bricks, they came into the construction trailer to get their check. I explained that this was a holiday and the mail would not be delivered today. I knew that they would finish soon and I had already requested their check to be mailed. "I want my money now," the masonry subcontractor told me. I explained the circumstances again. The contractor had five of his crew with him. There was one of my laborers in the office also. "Call the post office and get permission to come down and get the letter with the check in it," he demanded.

To help to calm him down, I called and talked with the postmaster. He obligingly checked to see if the letter was actually there. "Yes, the letter is here. It will be delivered tomorrow," he told me. I explained, to them, what the postmaster has said.

The contractor said, "You see all of my men, we are going to take it out of your hide if we don't get paid today." I was trembling inside, but I tried to not let it show. "Alright, beat me up, do what you want to, it still does not get you your money, today. I listen to some threats and lots of cursing. Eventfully, they accepted the fact that it was impossible to get their money, right now.

They sat there a few minutes and one of the guys said, "Boss, what are we having for lunch?" He answered, "I don't know about the rest of you, but looks like I am going to have to eat some crow."

Stores in Tennessee

Chapter Four
Stores in Tennessee

When the jobs in Charlotte were winding down they sent me to Greenville, TN. East Tennessee is beautiful country. I love the rolling hills.

The building went well. The Editor of the local newspaper wrote an article about the store being built. He said, "A watched pot never boils until they started building the Hardees Restaurant." This fast construction was something new for the small Tennessee town.

The weather was unpredictable. The skies would be sunshine and suddenly black clouds and storms would come across the mountains and a downpour of rain within minutes.

The area was subject to flooding. While we were there we had a flood that caused the waters to rise about two feet in front of the store.

While building the store in Greeneville, I became friends with a Chiropractor who lived and had an office next door. I wife and I visited them often through the later years.

After this job I went to Elizabethton which is about 40 miles away.

When I got there the lot had three good size houses and a small three bedroom house. My first job was to get the houses moved or torn down.

The three larger houses were moved to new locations. An elderly lady live in the small house alone.

She was served with notice to vacate.

She didn't move.

I knocked on her door and told her the house was going to be torn down. She said she was waiting for her son to move her things.

Several attempts were made to get her to move. Nothing happened. The grading company had cleared the property with exception to her house.

The home office was getting tired of sending me warning to get her out of the house. I got a message from Jay Hammond that said Richardson is demanding that she vacate the house.

I had to do something. I instructed the dozer operator to get on the farther side of the property and head toward her house. I told him to drive in the slowest speed possible and not stop for anything.

I knocked on her door and asked her to come out on the porch. I said, "That dozer is coming to smash this house. It will take him a few minutes to get here and there is nothing I can do to stop him."

She called her son and told him. He was there with his pickup and had her out within minutes. Forty-five minutes from the time I gave instructions to the dozer operator the house was flattened and ready to haul away.

Sometimes it takes drastic measures. Would I have allowed them the destroy her house with her in it? Of course not. She just needed some motivation.

I remember going to the small restaurant across the street. One day they had Bar-B-que on the menu. I asked the waitress if the Bar-B-que was good. She said, "It ought to be, we opened a new can this morning."

The weather here was interesting. I had a crew cleaning the parking lot. There was a bank across the street with a temperature sign. We noticed that it was getting cooler. The sun was shining so we kept working. We had a sudden thunderstorm that lasted a short while. As the temperature dropped it started to sleet. As the temperature reached 33 degrees it came a beautiful snow. All these different degrees of weather came with a few hours.

I had an assistant who was from the mid-west. He was a great worker. The company paid our expenses so he saved most of his pay. There was a car dealer with a promotion nearby. They had a beautiful older model of a Cadillac and the sign said the price would drop every hour until the car is sold. Bill watched the price for several hours. When it got down to what he wanted to pay he bought it.

He told me, "I have a great car and a thousand dollars in my pocket, it's time for me to move on." I hated losing such a good worker, but I had to tell him goodbye.

Bill was a great guy. He kept my boots polished and shined. I asked him why he did it and he said, "I like the feel of leather."

Morristown, Tennessee

Chapter Five
Morristown, Tennessee

Several interesting things happened while the store in Morristown was being built.

My brother Jerry was the superintendent on the job. Often when I was between stores I visited other construction sites to check their progress.

If you ever worked with Spartan Food System you know that employees were taught to call their manager or supervisor mister.

One day while the concrete parking lot was being poured everyone was working hard when Jerry Richardson drove up. He walked around to see the progress.

A fairly new employee saw him and yelled, "Hey Jerry. Where is Charlie? My Richardson replied, "I really don't know where he is today, but when I see him I will get his schedule and see that you get a copy of it."

It so happened that Jay Hammond who was Vice President and in charge of all construction was on the job at the same time and heard the conversation. The employee got a scolding that I am sure he still remembers.

Another interesting event was when the equipment was being installed Harold Jackson from Alabama was on the job training the equipment people about refrigeration. Late one evening several of us went to dinner at a downtown restaurant.

Morristown had double sidewalks, which was something very unusual. I asked Harold Jackson about it. He replied very quickly, "Don't say anything about those double sidewalks to anyone in town. Being curious, I asked why.

He said when he first came into town he asks an elderly man about the sidewalks and he replied, "What the hell are you doing trying to start another war?" Harold asked him why he was so touchy about the sidewalks. He answered, Them damn slabs of concrete have been friction between the residents and city management since the day they decided to do it."

Fishing in Bahamas

Chapter Six
Fishing Trip

When the current rush of store openings slowed down, Mr. Richardson told four of us that he was going to reward us with a three-day trip to the Bahamas.

Jay Hammond was a pilot and owed a four seat single engine plane. We got to the airport about 5:00 am and was ready to take off. Suddenly there was a knock on the window and Richardson had a bag of refreshments and bid us a pleasant flight. He was strict and at times considered ruthless but he had a pleasant and generous side.

We landed in Fort Lauderdale to get clearance to continue the flight. Soon we were over the Atlantic Ocean with no land in sight. No one offered any concerns, but there must have been thoughts of flying over the Atlantic with one engine.

We landed on one of the Keys, which is a small island, along the Grand Bahamas. The landing field was short and unpaved. When we landed an old rusted out station wagon met us and the driver explained that he was the only taxi on the island.

We drove a few miles to the fishing village where there was a modern motel and fishing boats for rent.

We inquired about a boat that we could live on for three days. We were told that all the boats are out except one that the captain is rebuilding the engine. While we waited for him to finish we shopped for food and supplies to last three days on the boat.

Within a few hours, he announced that our boat was ready. We loaded and set out to find a good fishing spot.

The captain carried us to a quite spot and said that this is the best place to fish. There were only three rod and reels on board. One of the guys told us that he didn't need one. He tied a fishing line on a hook and dropped it over the side. About an hour later he caught a 43-pound grouper. That was the biggest fish caught on the trip.

On the third day, our food was all gone. We saw a shack by the shore with a crudely painted sign that said, restaurant. We docked and went inside. The place was dirty and empty. Shortly a man came running and said, "Do you want to eat?" We told him yes and he said that he will have to go and hire a cook.

While he was gone we decided to leave. The captain went down little ways and docked until we decided what to do about food.

Olin Thompson, who was a restaurant owner before coming to Spartan Foods said, "Let me see what I can find. There must be something on the boat we can eat." He found a can of Spam and a box of oatmeal. He rolled the Spam in oatmeal and fried it. We eat it for Supper. That was over 40 years ago and I haven't wanted Spam since.

Later we went back to the marina and got a good meal at the motel.

There was a fishing contest going on. I asked, "What do they do with all these big fish when the contest is over." The answer was, Go in the restaurant tonight and you will see."

I didn't fish very much, I started getting sick. I didn't really know why. Later, I learned that my ankles

Hickory, North Carolina

Chapter Seven
Hickory, NC

The building in Hickory was some obstacles from the beginning.

First we had to appear before the county council to get special permission. It was granted without a fight. This was one of the old pagoda style buildings that had to be totally remodeled.

Part ways through the job my best carpenter fell from the roof and broke his back. That left me personally responsible for finishing the carpentry work, including Formica in the manager's office.

Also during the job I stepped on a board that had a nail in it. The nail went through the sole of my boots and good ways into my foot.

It was very difficult to walk. I cut a block of wood and taped it my boot to keep the pressure off the injury. It was a couple days before I could get to the doctor. By the it was badly infected.

Across town, another superintendent was building a new store. Toward the end of the job Jay Hammond told me they needed him in Alabama and I would have to finish the job. That made me running two jobs at the same time.

I checked his progress and he was a month behind schedule. I was able to catch up the schedule and finished on time, except one item. The electrician finished but didn't have the labels with him to put on the breakers in the electrical panel box. That was done early the next morning.

My remodel job was finished on schedule.

Building Hardees Restaurants

Alabama Stores

Chapter Eight
Alabama Stores

A large number of stores were built in the state of Alabama. When they were completed they all discovered a problem.

There was a problem with the exhaust system. Actually, the exhaust was so strong that it held the doors open. There was not enough "Make-up" air.

A design was drawn for a box to be placed in the ceiling adjacent to the hood.

I took an assistant with me and we stopped in

Florence, AL to get a shop to build the boxes. When they got all of them finished we loaded and headed across the state.

We worked at night and drove the next morning to the next location.

It was a grueling job. On one occasion my assistant was driving and he swung to the left side of the road. I said, "What are you doing?" He said, "I am passing that car." There was not another car on the road. I knew then that he had lost too much sleep and I took the wheel until he was awake enough to drive.

We got the job done.

Spartanburg

West Main

Chapter Nine

Spartanburg

I was proud of all the restaurants I built, but one was really special. The store in Spartanburg on West Main Street was to be completely renovated.

The building was the old Pagoda style, with walk-up windows. It was to be converted to the new design, with the orange facade. The job was assigned to me.

The job called for tearing out most of the inside, building new brick walls and adding dining space. This was the only building that I closed during remodeling. The manager closed the business on Sunday evening. I was standing by with a crew of workers.

First, we took all the equipment out of the kitchen. The laborers got started breaking down the partition walls. I had a jackhammer and compressor ready. Portions of the floor were broken out.

The plumbers came in and relocated the rough-in for the plumbing. The electricians had to relocate all the underground wiring.

When that was done we poured the concrete floors. I laid the block walls. The ceramic tile contractor came in and laid the tile on the floors and walls. A new ceiling had to be put in. Then, the electricians and plumbers came back and did their finish work.

We built the new roof to tie in with the old style roofing. New equipment was installed. The restaurant re-opened for business, on Thursday of the same week. Yes, you read it right. The business was closed only four days.

At one point, Jerry Richardson, rode by the job, took a look and kept going. He went back to the office and went straight to Jay Hammond's office. With an obvious look of frustration, he said, "I went by the job and Smith has got both ends of the building torn out and it is late in the evening. Do you realize the security problems?" Hammond said with confidence, "Smith knows what he's doing. Leave him alone."

On Thursday, the store was reopened. Do you realize that we did all that construction in four days?

An impossible task was done.

Snow Storm

Snow Storm

Chapter Ten
The Snow Storm

I was assigned to work a couple weeks in middle Tennessee while the superintendent was on vacation.

This was the middle of December. There were several others stores being built at the same time. We were told if we would work until Christmas eve they would fly us home.

Jay Hammond had bought a six-passenger plane. We met him at the airport about 1:00. The weather looked good and we expected to be home soon.

Soon after take-off we were told to land in Chatta-nooga; all planes were being grounded. A snow and freeze front was coming through.

We spent five hours at the airport listening to stories about flying in freezing weather.

Then, we got clearance to go as far as Atlanta. Reaching the Atlanta area we got clearance to go to Athens and land.

Approaching Athens, they said we could go as far as Anderson and we would be grounded. Hammond asked, "What other planes are in the area?" They said there is only one other plane within a hundred miles and it was a transport which was equipped with deicers.

The snow was coming down hard and the outside temperature was 31. Hammond said, "Let's take a vote. Do we trust that the temperature will not fall one degree and go home for Christmas." The vote went go home.

We reached the downtown airport in Spartanburg a few minutes before midnight. That was a dangerous decision and I do not recommend anyone doing that again.

We were glad to be home for Christmas.

An Expensive Error

ts

Chapter Eleven
An Expensive Error

Sammy Williams was the superintendent on the job in Columbia, Tennessee. The job was on schedule. Operations had ordered the food and was completing their training.

Jay Hammond decided to fly up there the day before opening. As usual, he flew over the job site before landing.

He was in shock when he saw what was going on.

The plumber had a ditch across the entire parking lot. Williams did not notify the office that there was a plumbing problem. He decided that he would get it fixed before the office knew about it.

Hammond went to the airport and landed, but he was so upset that he forgot to lower the landing gear.

It destroyed the entire underneath of the plane.

Fripp Island

Chapter Twelve

Fripp Island

Spartan had a house at Fripp Island where training meetings were held. The house was also used for management personnel to vacation. The house was called the CJD house, which is Charlie Bradshaw, Jerry Richardson, and Dick Hardee.

My family had the privilege of spending several weekends during my time with Spartan.

One was very memorable. It was mine and Johnnie's anniversary. We spent the week there with our five children. On Friday night, we decided to go to the club for a steak dinner.

Leaving the CJD house, we noticed that Charlie Bradshaw, who was the Chairman of the Board of Spartan Food System was also at Fripp. The Bradshaw's owned a separate house a few doors from the CJD house.

Mr. Bradshaw and his wife were in the yard. We stopped to say hello went on to the club house.

When we finished eating the waitress said, "Your bill is already paid." We asked who paid it and she told us that Mr. Bradshaw called and put it on his account.

Charlie Bradshaw was a great guy.

In every event at Fripp when the management met for a weekend there was always time for sports.

One time we were divided into two teams; red and white tee shirts. We did a variety of competitions. One was push ups and pull ups on the bar. When it came my time I did a pull ups touched my chin on the bar. Mr. Richardson stopped me. He said, "You are doing it wrong. Your head has to come in front of the bar." I had never done that before. I tried and did one pull up. I made up for it when we did the push ups.

We played softball. I saw something never seen in real life; it was like in the movies. Jay Hammond ran for the ball and he failed to see the pond behind him. It was the most amazing thing I have ever seen. It appeared that he walked on top of the water and didn't sink until he stopped.

We played volleyball. Jay Hammond and Jerry Richardson chose the others to play on their team. One time there was a strong argument between Hammond and Richardson as to where the ball landed. One said it was inside and the other said it was outside. Richardson finally said, "Here is what we will do. We'll let Smith make the call and we will abide by it." I thought, seems like forever and then I said, The ball hit on the line. Richardson said That's final and it was never mentioned again.

Let in the evening I sat on the screened porch and talked with Mr. Bradshaw. He told me about the companies goals and opportunities they had and turned down. It was a great weekend.

On a separate weekend about half way through someone came from the clubhouse with a message. (The CJD house didn't have a telephone.) Mr. Hammond called me aside and told me that my dad had an accident and was in the hospital. I flew down with Hammond and Olin Thompson. I didn't know how I was going to get home. Mr. Richardson said, "Take my car and my chauffeur and use them as long as you need them."

Athens, Alabama

Chapter Thirteen
Athens, Alabama

My last store with Spartan Food System was in Athens, Alabama. There were some challenging moments during the finish of the job, that were frustrating.

It was time for the light fixtures to be delivered, but they didn't come. I called the lighting supplier and he said, "The fixtures you are using are manufactured in Italy and we are out of them." He went on to say, "The job in Mississippi has some left over, I will call and have them delivered to you." I thanked him for his help.

After five days, the fixtures didn't come. I called the supplier again, "Where are my fixtures," I asked? "Raymond, I am sorry, they made a mistake and sent the fixtures back here to the warehouse. I will get them on the next truck coming your way and you should have them in about five days."

I was getting hot under the collar but tried to stay calm. "That's not good enough this job is scheduled to finish in three days. I have never been late with a job and I won't be late with this one," I told him.

The manager of the lighting company saw that I was determined. He said, "Can you meet the truck half way if I send them on our truck?" "Yes, I can," I told him. "Okay, meet the truck at the intersection of I-85 and 285, in Atlanta, at 10:00 tomorrow morning," He instructed me.

I was apprehensive about driving to Atlanta. I had

already worked two days and a night, without sleep. After working that many hours, straight, without sleep, on another job, I laid down on a stack of sheetrock and dozed off. When I awoke, one of the laborers said, "Boss, we thought you were dead"

Even with a lack of rest, to keep my reputation, I was willing to make the four-hour trip.

At 10:00, I was sitting in a Waffle House, drinking coffee, waiting for the truck. Shortly, I saw the one-ton stake body truck with the company's name on it. I also saw, there were no light fixtures on the truck. The driver made the cloverleaf circle and pulled into the Waffle House parking lot. I yelled at the driver, "Where are my light fixtures?" The driver looking surprised said, "The boss didn't say anything about any light fixtures. He just said gas up the truck and meet you here."

I was fit to be tied. I got on the phone with the

manager and said, "WHAT HAPPENED TO MY LIGHT FIXTURES?" The manager very apologetically said I have already discovered the problem. Since it's my fault if you will stay where you are, I will put the fixtures in my station wagon and bring them to you personally." I agreed. What else could I do?

In one hour and forty-five minutes, the station wagon pulled into the Waffle House parking lot.

I got back to the job and the electrician finished his part of the contract. The job was completed on time.

Conclusion

I worked exactly four years with Spartan Food System. It was a great experience. I loved the people I was working for.

I felt that I could earn more money in my own construction company. When I gave Jay Hammond my two weeks notice he said, "Smith I would try to talk you into saying, but knowing you when you make up you mind to do something, there is no use arguing.

While with the company I built or totaled remodeled 23 stores. I worked 47 to 110 hours a week when remodeling. I was on straight salary and did not earn anything extra for the overtime.

A few weeks after leaving I got a check which read, "Retirement paid in full." I was excited until I read the amount. It was $43.00. I learned later that the requirement to earn monthly retirement checks was five years.

See all of Raymond E. Smith's books;